Introduction to Singapore

The Republic of Singapore stands today as an example of what can be achieved in a very short time by people with single-minded dedication and national unity. A tiny nation in both population (four million) and area (648 square kilometres) terms, Singapore's presence and stature are much greater than these statistics would lead observers to expect.

In just thirty-five years Singapore has developed from a former British colony and trading port into the key financial, shipping and technology centre for Southeast Asia. The huge problems of racial tension, poverty and poor environment that existed in the 1960s have been conquered to a large extent.

In the early twenty-first century Singapore is experiencing a slowing down of its phenomenal growth. Even so, it remains an economic powerhouse in the Asia–Pacific region. It is expected that financial services and high-technology research and manufacturing will dominate its future.

As life becomes more prosperous for Singaporeans, it is likely some social problems will develop as they have done in European societies.

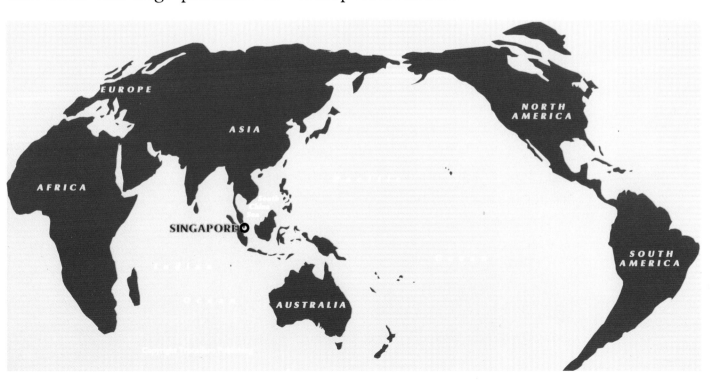

Government structure

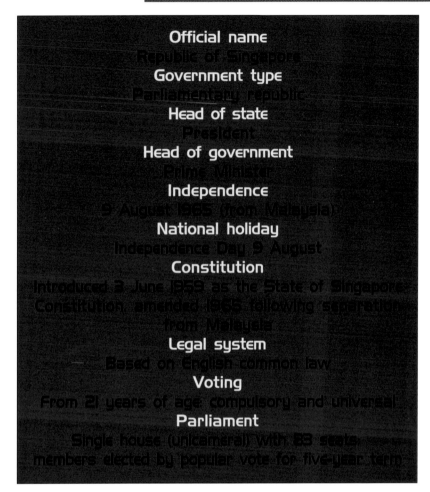

Official name
Republic of Singapore
Government type
Parliamentary republic
Head of state
President
Head of government
Prime Minister
Independence
9 August 1965 (from Malaysia)
National holiday
Independence Day 9 August
Constitution
Introduced 3 June 1959 as the State of Singapore
Constitution, amended 1965 following separation
from Malaysia
Legal system
Based on English common law
Voting
From 21 years of age compulsory and universal
Parliament
Single house (unicameral) with 83 seats;
members elected by popular vote for five-year term

Singapore is a republic and a member of the Commonwealth of Nations. Its Parliament was originally based upon the British Westminster system; however, it has been adapted over the years to suit local conditions. The head of state is the president, who, since 1993, is elected by popular vote.

The president resides at the Istana, previously Government House, the residence of British governors in the colonial period.

The Parliament meets at Parliament House in High Street.

The Singaporean legal system, while based on English law, does not have trial by jury. It relies instead on individual judges ruling on cases. The death penalty is still used, particularly for drug trafficking offences. Executions are carried out regularly at Changi Prison.

In 1993, for the first time, Singaporeans were able to vote for the office of President of the Republic. Previous presidents since 1959 had been appointed by the government.

Leading Singapore

Since the 1970s the People's Action Party (PAP) has had a virtual stranglehold on Singapore's Parliament. Its long domination has resulted in a system of government that many, both inside and outside the country,

THE NATIONAL PLEDGE

We, the citizens of Singapore, pledge ourselves as one united people, regardless of race, language or religion, to build a democratic society based on justice and equality so as to achieve happiness, prosperity and progress for our nation.

find very oppressive. Critics of the government often find themselves involved in expensive court procedures. Some Singaporeans argue that their economic prosperity has been at the expense of their freedom to speak or to criticise without fear.

On the positive side, life for most Singaporeans has improved remarkably since the 1960s. Much of this can be attributed to the PAP under the dynamic and uncompromising leadership of Lee Kuan Yew, prime minister from 1959 to 1990.

After the failure of the union with Malaysia, Prime Minister Lee was able to energise the new nation and unite the people in an economic and social strategy that is much-admired around the world. Singapore today is a first world nation. Its citizens enjoy world-class civic amenities and all have access to a minimum standard of housing and all basic social services. Education facilities are excellent. The Singapore business community is relatively corruption-free and standards are generally very high.

Lee has become well known for his criticisms of Western culture and his promotion of 'Asian values'. A charismatic leader, he won the elections in 1959 in partnership with the Communist Party. Although he broke with the communists soon afterwards, for a number of years in the early 1960s he was regarded as a communist sympathiser.

When Lee stood down from the leadership on 28 November 1990, his replacement was Goh Chok Tong. He remains a member of the government, having the office of Special Minister. Lee's influence continues to be felt today.

www.sources

www.gov.sg
Official Singapore government site

www.sg/govern.html
Numerous links to government sites

www.scholars.nus.edu.sg/landow/post/singapore/government/leekuanyew/leekuanyewov.html
Lee Kuan Yew biographical details

Transport

Occupying a small area, Singapore has been able to follow a policy of integrated and well-planned transport development. The past twenty years have seen huge advances in public transport, aviation and shipping. Also, while road transport facilities are excellent, official policies discourage private car use in favour of public transport. The well-planned creation of housing estates, with public transport as an inbuilt factor, has been a key to this.

Public transport

Public transport is primarily by bus and train, with light rail also being developed recently. The Mass Rapid Transit

An MRT train

PUBLIC TRANSPORT
MRT
103 trains, each with 6 cars
1 101 880 daily trips
by commuters

BUSES
3517 buses
3 079 000 daily trips
by commuters

(MRT) system, which began operations in 1987, is a highly efficient commuter railway using multi-carriage, air-conditioned electric trains. MRT lines run both under the city streets and on elevated viaducts through the suburbs. The Light Rail Transit (LRT) system being constructed in a number of areas feeds passengers to the MRT. The 49-station MRT system will be extended to Changi Airport in 2002.

Virtually all parts of Singapore are served by buses operated by Singapore Bus Services or Trans-Island Bus Services. All routes and fares are under the control of the government's Public Transport Council. Most buses are air-conditioned, and electronic signs at bus stops advise waiting passengers when the next service will arrive.

Car usage

While most Singaporeans aspire to car ownership, the nation has a firm policy of controlling the number of vehicles on its roads. This is done to avoid the severe traffic congestion and pollution that many other Asian cities suffer.

Before obtaining a car, Singaporeans must bid for a Certificate of Entitlement (COE). The COE entitles them to purchase a car, which will be very expensive by the standards of most countries. Car prices are kept high by the government, through heavy taxes and import duties, to suppress vehicle numbers.

Backing up these measures is the Electronic Road Pricing (ERP) system, under which all cars are fitted with electronic monitors.

Vehicle traffic in the Orchard Road shopping district

SCOTT BRODIE

When the car uses a particular road or motorway, electronic sensors charge the owner a fee.

Aviation

Singapore's commercial aviation is all international, there are no domestic services. Airline operations are based around Changi Airport, which opened in the early 1980s. Built partly on reclaimed land, Changi is large, modern, spacious, efficient and easy for passengers to use. There

A Singapore Airlines Boeing 747 landing at Changi Airport

SINGAPORE AIRLINES

MRT Routes

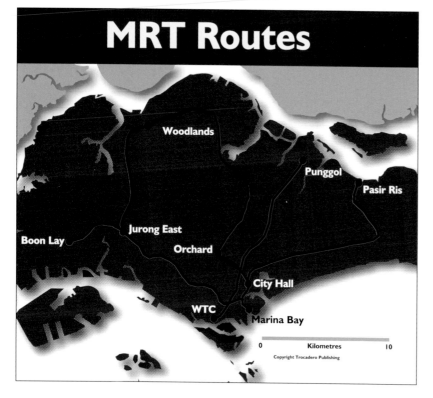

Woodlands

Punggol

Pasir Ris

Jurong East

Boon Lay

Orchard

City Hall

WTC

Marina Bay

0   Kilometres   10

Copyright Trocadero Publishing

region. Aircraft from more than fifty airlines arrive and depart regularly on scheduled services. Airlines such as Qantas use Changi as an interchange to enable passengers from various parts of Australia to link up with flights to Europe and other parts of Asia.

Internationally the nation is represented by Singapore Airlines, which flies to most parts of the world. A smaller operator, Silk Air, flies to other destinations in the South-east Asian region. Singapore Airlines has followed a policy of regularly upgrading its fleet of aircraft as well as maintaining high standards of passenger care.

are two large terminal buildings, with a third to open in 2006.

The government is attempting to develop Changi further as a major aviation centre in Asia. This involves expanding existing aircraft maintenance services, possibly even to the extent of building aircraft or their components.

Changi, with its user-friendly facilities, is a major airport for the

Flights to 145 cities in 50 countries

3300 weekly flights

1.7 million tonnes of freight per year

The jinrickshaw is one form of transport that has long since disappeared from Singapore's streets

On the northern side of the island the Sembawang facility is a large and modern ship repair and maintenance centre. Sembawang was developed from the large King George V dry dock built by Britain's Royal Navy in the 1930s.

Loading a container ship by night

Shipping

When it comes to total tonnage of goods handled, Singapore is the world's largest port, just beating Hong Kong. A staggering 145 000 ships pass through the Port of Singapore each year, carrying in excess of 900 million tonnes of cargo. Ships sail from Singapore to more than 400 ports around the world.

Located on the south-western and western coasts of the island, Singapore's ports are among the most modern in the world. The Pasir Panjang terminal has been upgraded to handle mega-cargo ships that carry more than 6000 containers at a time.

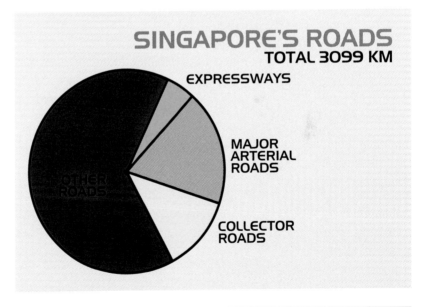

SINGAPORE'S ROADS
TOTAL 3099 KM
EXPRESSWAYS
MAJOR ARTERIAL ROADS
COLLECTOR ROADS
OTHER ROADS

WWW.SOURCES
www.ptc.gov.sg/links.htm
Links to all Singapore public transport sites

www.singaporeair.com
Singapore Airlines official site

www.changi.airport.com.sg
Changi Airport official site

www.sembawang.per.sg
History of Sembawang dockyard

Communications

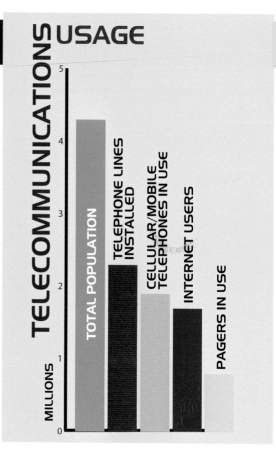

TELECOMMUNICATIONS USAGE

MILLIONS

- TOTAL POPULATION
- TELEPHONE LINES INSTALLED
- CELLULAR/MOBILE TELEPHONES IN USE
- INTERNET USERS
- PAGERS IN USE

Telecommunications are vitally important to the development of Singapore. Official policies are geared to providing the latest possible systems for industry and private consumers, through both voice and internet connections. The intention is to make Singapore an international hub for electronic communications, using the talents of entrepreneurs and the local workforce.

A key part of this policy is the creation of Singapore ONE, a national broadband network for offices, homes and schools. Singapore ONE enables access to a range of multimedia applications and services at a higher speed than the internet. It also allows the government to maintain closer control over internet traffic than in most countries. The system, connected to homes, offices, schools, public libraries and public kiosks around the island, currently has approximately 260 000 users.

Mobile telephones — or handphones, as Singaporeans call them — are popular and in widespread use for both voice and data transmissions. Around seventy-five per cent of the population have mobile telephones. Pagers also remain popular for business and personal use, with in excess of 800 000 subscribers. There are also 1.9 million fixed, or conventional, telephone lines.

Teaching of information technology has a high priority. By 2003 it is expected that all school leavers will have had access to IT training. Currently, more than 90 000 people are employed directly in the various IT industries in Singapore, with 2500 graduates in the field entering the workforce each year.

www.sources

www.singtel.com
Singapore Telecom

www.phonebook.com.sg
Singapore telephone directory

www.ida.gov.sg
Infocomm Development Authority

Industry

EXPORTS
WHERE SINGAPORE SENDS ITS EXPORTS

GERMANY
SOUTH KOREA
CHINA
NETHERLANDS
UK
THAILAND
TAIWAN
JAPAN
HONG KONG

OTHERS
USA
MALAYSIA

Singapore has very little primary industry. What exists is mostly market gardening to serve the local community. The nation's real power lies in its secondary industries. The government for

SINGAPORE'S MAIN INDUSTRIES
electronics
chemicals
financial services
oil drilling equipment
petroleum refining
rubber processing
rubber products
processed food
beverages
ship repair
entrepôt trade
biotechnology

Singapore contrasts — a modern office tower dwarfs a more traditional commercial building

SCOTT BRODIE

IMPORTS
WHERE SINGAPORE'S IMPORTS COME FROM

OTHERS
USA
SAUDI ARABIA
GERMANY
TAIWAN
JAPAN
CHINA
THAILAND
MALAYSIA

production of high-technology components and finished goods. These range from special-purpose machines to home electronic equipment. Also, on the research and development front, Singapore has become a leader in the development of biotechnology.

One of the most important and diverse heavy industries is the processing of rubber, grown in neighbouring Malaysia, into a

many years promoted a particular range of industries that it believed best suited Singapore's situation. Older style industries have given way to those that use a higher degree of technology. In many cases Singapore provides the creative and design processes for goods that are then manufactured elsewhere in Asia.

There is a booming electronics industry, in both design and

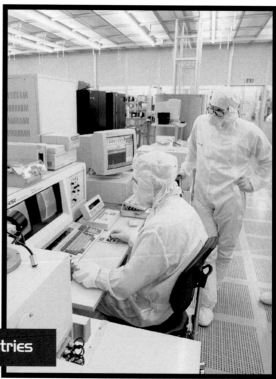

Singapore is a leader in high-technology industries

SINGAPORE'S EXPORTS

Exports **US$137 billion**
Main exports **Machinery and equipment, electronics, chemicals, mineral fuels**

SINGAPORE'S IMPORTS

Imports **US$127 billion**
Main imports **Machinery and equipment, mineral fuels, chemicals, foodstuffs**

wide range of products. With the large Sembawang complex as a base, Singapore has also become a major centre for ship repair and maintenance procedures. In the same vein is construction of oil-drilling rigs for use in exploration in the surrounding oceans.

Printing is one of the industries on which
Singapore built its industrial power

Manufacturing aside, Singapore is also renowned as a financial centre for Asia. Government incentives have encouraged world financial institutions to locate their regional offices here. A comprehensive legal structure and the absence of corruption make Singapore an attractive place for such organisations to be located. More than thirty-five per cent of the workforce is engaged in financial and business services.

Printing is one of the industries on which Singapore built its industrial power

This factory at Jurong was typical of the sort of manufacturing plant that came to Singapore from the 1960s onwards

The large Sembawang shipyard was originally part of the Royal Navy base

www.sources

www.sci.org.sg
Singapore Confederation of Industry
www.singstat.gov.sg/STATS/yos13.pdf
Official manufacturing statistics

Geography, environment and climate

Singapore's high rainfall gives the island nation lush vegetation everywhere

Singapore island is mostly low lying, rising on the southern side to a low plateau. The lowest point is sea level; the highest point is 165 metres, at Bukit Timah. With continuing development, the area of forest and woodland has dropped to five per cent of the

land mass. About six per cent of the island is given over to agriculture, principally market gardens.

Located close to the equator, Singapore has a tropical climate. It is hot and humid all year round, with heavy rainfall on most days, often in the form of a late afternoon thunderstorm. The island is affected by two monsoon seasons,

SINGAPORE'S RAINFALL

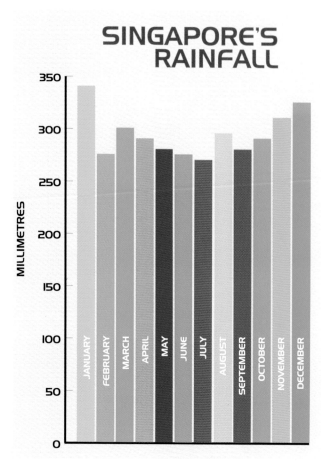

MILLIMETRES

SINGAPORE'S SIZE
Area **647.5** sq. km
Coastline **193** km

June–September and December–March. The steamy conditions are overcome by widespread use of air-conditioning in offices, homes and vehicles.

Because of its policy of limiting car ownership, Singapore is less affected by exhaust emission pollution than most other Asian countries; however, it does suffer some industrial pollution. In recent years the burning of forests for land clearance in Indonesia has seen the island blanketed in smoke haze on some days. The small land area also presents problems with the disposal of waste by landfill methods.

SINGAPORE'S LOCATION
Latitude 1°22'N
Longitude 103°48'E

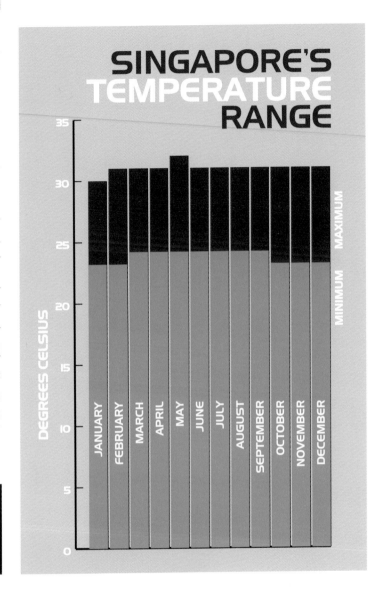

SINGAPORE'S TEMPERATURE RANGE

DEGREES CELSIUS

MAXIMUM

MINIMUM

JANUARY · FEBRUARY · MARCH · APRIL · MAY · JUNE · JULY · AUGUST · SEPTEMBER · OCTOBER · NOVEMBER · DECEMBER

www.sources
geography.miningco.com/library/maps/blsingapore.htm
Geographical details and maps

www.scholars.nus.edu.sg/landow/post/singapore/
literature/misc/descript.html
Descriptions of Singapore's climate

www.photius.com/wfb2000/countries/singapore/
singapore_geography.html
Details of climate and geography

www.sec.org.sg
Singapore Environment Council

Peoples and daily life

SINGAPORE'S ETHNIC MIX

OTHERS

INDIAN

MALAY

CHINESE

Chinese arrivals were mostly from three regions of China: the Hokkien from Fujian; the Cantonese, Teochew and Hakka from Guangdong; and Hainanese from Hainan Island. At the time of Raffles' arrival, China was going through political convulsions as opposition grew to the Qing Dynasty's rule. Many Chinese set up business, with some securing lucrative positions as intermediaries between European and Asian traders.

Singaporeans today are almost all descended from immigrants, most of whom came to the island after Stamford Raffles established the British trading post in 1819. The few inhabitants who preceded him were mostly Malay or Chinese. The population increased rapidly once word passed around about the new opportunities for profit. Those who came to Singapore did so with the intention of making their money and returning home, but many stayed permanently.

Unique Singapore architecture in the Orchard Road shopping and entertainment district

As the settlement grew, many Malays crossed the Johor Strait to obtain work. They were joined by people from various parts of India, but predominantly Madras and Negapatam. Arab traders — whose ancestors had introduced Islam to Malaya — were also prominent in Singapore trading circles. From across the Malacca Straits came Javanese and Boyanese (from Bawean Island).

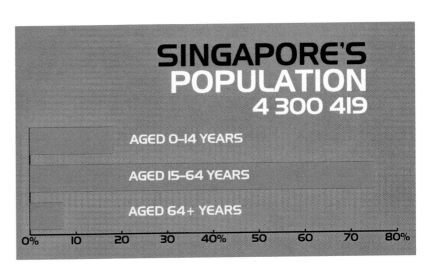

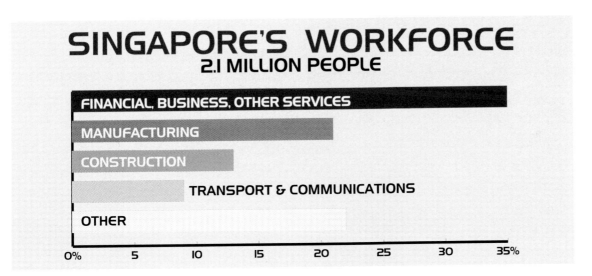

Also drawn by the potential for trade were British, American and Portuguese entrepreneurs. Initially most European-owned trading houses specialised in exporting spices to Europe and importing a wide range of manufactured goods for Singaporeans to purchase. British officials were sent to Singapore to manage the business of the East India Company and to administer the settlement.

Today, most Singaporeans belong to one of three major cultural groups: Chinese, Malay or Indian. There is also a minority European grouping. Chinese-Singaporeans are the largest group,

LANGUAGES
Chinese (official)
Malay (official and national)
Tamil (official)
English (official)

LOCHMAN TRANSPARENCIES — WADE HUGHES

An array of fresh vegeatables in a Singapore street market

most Singaporeans is similar to that in many European countries. The working week for most is Monday to Friday, although some also work on Saturdays. The majority live in high-rise apartments on specially developed estates across the island. Most commute to work by bus or on the highly efficient MRT rail system.

Outside working hours Singaporeans like to indulge in a wide range of recreations, including playing or watching sport, going to movies, socialising with their friends, and shopping. There are many opportunities for shopping in Singapore, with most stores open until at least nine o'clock each evening. Singaporeans also love to eat out, enjoying a vast range of cuisines in eating places that range from simple outdoor 'hawker stalls' to the most lavish and expensive restaurants.

with seventy-six per cent of the population; Malay-Singaporeans make up fifteen per cent; and Indian-Singaporeans six per cent.

Singapore is a highly urbanised society. As there is very little agricultural activity, most food is imported. The highly educated workforce is primarily engaged in the manufacturing industry or service activities. Daily life for

LONELY PLANET IMAGES — RICHARD I'ANSON

Restaurants and retail outlets in renovated shophouses of Boat Quay, on the Singapore River

Singapore's housing problems were acute after World War II — the scene below was typical of housing in 1946 — but by the 1980s large new estates (right) had been constructed for the population

SCOTT BRODIE

The largest provider of housing in Singapore is the government's Housing and Development Board (HDB). Around eighty-six per cent of Singaporeans live in high-rise apartments owned and managed by the HDB. The primary role of the Board is to ensure all Singaporeans have access to affordable accommodation. It also operates schemes that enable people to purchase their apartments. Housing estates are regularly upgraded to avoid their deterioration into unattractive living environments.

www.sources

www.hdb.gov.sg
Housing & Development Board

www.expatsingapore.com
Life in Singapore for expatriates

windoshop.com/sin/wstips.html
Guide to shopping in Singapore

www.lib.nus.edu.sg/clb/sub/libsinga.html
Guide to libraries in Singapore

www.happening.com.sg
Guide to entertainment in Singapore

Food and cuisine

INDIAN FOODS

Chapati
flat whole-wheat bread

Dhosai
rice flour and lentil pancake

Gulam jamun
cream cheese balls in syrup

Kulfi
rich milk and nut dessert

Prata
crisp crusty pancake served
with curry gravy

Puri
deep-fried bread served
with potato curry

Samosa
triangular snack filled with
potatoes or meat

Teh-halia
ginger tea

Thairu
yoghurt

Vada
savoury lentil doughnut

Singapore's mix of ethnic cultures has also led to a huge range of foods being available in the island nation. Probably the most visible are the various strands of Chinese cuisine. Particularly popular dishes in Singapore are dim sum, chilli chicken, Hainanese chicken rice, Peking duck, Teochew porridge and steamboat.

The Indian community is famous for fish-head curry, although this is a Singaporean creation rather than one brought from India. The cooking styles of both northern and southern India are available: the southern tends to be hot and spicy, the northern leans more towards a subtler blending of spices and other ingredients. Some favourites in Singapore are biriyani, gulab jamun, mutton korma and masala thosai.

The nearest Singapore comes to its own unique cuisine is Peranakan, also known as Nonya. As would be expected, Peranakan takes the best of Chinese and Malay foods and flavours, blending them in a unique style. The key ingredients are chilli, belachan (shrimp paste) and coconut milk, and the most famous dishes are buah keluak, itek tim and nonya kueh.

While vegetarianism is not widespread in the Singapore community, there are some Buddhists and a large number of Indian-Singaporeans who prefer this style of food. For many Hindus, vegetarianism stems from the belief that all animal life is to be revered. In particular, the cow is seen as a holy animal because it provides milk, helps work the fields, and provides transport.

As well as using their own distinct cuisine, Malay-Singaporeans

A selection from the vast array of food available in Singapore

have perfected various blends of Malay with Thai and Indonesian cooking. They are particularly skilled in the use of coconut milk sauces and belachan. This dried shrimp paste is mixed with chilli to create sambal belachan, a real favourite in the community. Other popular dishes include beef rendang, nasi padang, soto ayam and mee goreng.

For all Singaporeans, seafood comes close to the top of the list of favourites. In the parkland areas along the motorway from Changi Airport to the CBD can be found numerous seafood restaurants that are always packed with diners. Singapore favourites include barbecued stingray, black pepper crab, chilli crab and deep-fried squid.

Western cuisines have also been enthusiastically adopted by Singaporeans, from the ubiquitous fast-food burger chains to the most lavish French restaurants. Particularly popular is Italian food, although it is prepared in a number of ways. There are restaurants and cafés with authentic Italian style, as well as those offering American and Australian variations.

In addition to eating well in their homes, Singaporeans are enthusiastic about dining out, often in large groups of family or friends. They are well catered for with a vast array of eating places. For inexpensive occasions they go to simple hawker's stalls where meals can be enjoyed in an outdoor setting. For a larger choice, there are thousands of restaurants offering every cuisine imaginable.

WWW.SOURCES

www.asiacuisine.com.sg
Guide to food and eating

www.expatsingapore.com/eating/restaurants.htm
Eating in Singapore

www.sg/food.html
Links to Singaporean food sites

Religion and beliefs

Muslim worshippers gather for Friday morning prayers at a mosque

Given the diversity of ethnic groups, it is to be expected that Singapore has a similar diversity of faiths. Singaporeans are free to practice the religion of their choice.

Chinese religions such as Buddhism, Taoism and Confucianism arrived on the island almost 1000 years ago with the early settlers. Arab traders and Malays from across the Johor Strait brought their Islamic faith. Indians who arrived in the past 200 years bolstered the Muslim congregation, while others introduced Hinduism and Sikhism to Singapore. Portuguese traders initially brought Christianity, later reinforced by British arrivals.

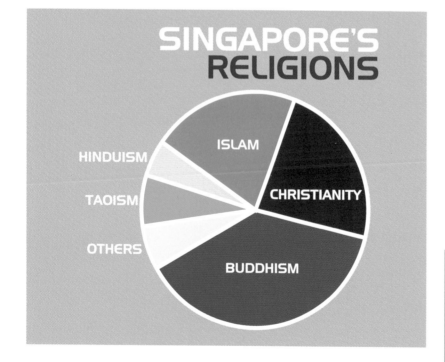

SINGAPORE'S RELIGIONS

HINDUISM
TAOISM
OTHERS
ISLAM
CHRISTIANITY
BUDDHISM

www.sources

www.np.edu.sg/sa/clubs/bs/Sing_link.htm
Links to Buddhist sites

www.njcnews.org/complink.htm
Links to Christian sites

www.muis.gov.sg
Islamic Religious Council of Singapore

www.heb.gov.sg
Hindu Endowments Board

History and politics

The early days

Early records of Singapore are few. Third century Chinese documents mention an island called Pu-luo-chung. In 1320 the Mongolian empire sent a delegation to Singapore to obtain elephants.

Ten years later Wang Dayuan, a visitor from China, found his fellow peoples already established on the island then known as Temasek or Tan-ma-hsi (sea town). It was an unattractive place, inhabited by gangs of pirates who raided trading ships heading for China.

At the end of the thirteenth century Temasek was under the control of the Hindu Sri Vijaya

LION CITY
Singapore, or Singapura, means Lion City. The usual explanation for this curious name is that early visitors claimed to have seen on the island a mythical beast that reminded them of a lion.

trading empire based on Sumatra. In 1377, when the Javanese Buddhist Majaphit empire went to war with Sri Vijaya, much of Temasek was destroyed.

The Kingdom of Siam (now Thailand) exploited this clash to seize control of the Malay Peninsula, including Temasek. By the sixteenth century Temasek had become well known to Portuguese trading ships.

The trading port of Singapore in the 1840s

THOMAS STAMFORD RAFFLES

Born 6 July 1781
aboard sailing ship *Ann*,
en route Jamaica–England
Died 5 July 1826, England

The coming of the British

The development of Singapore into a major trading centre began in the early nineteenth century. The British East India Company secured Prince of Wales Island (now Penang), off the western coast of the Malay Peninsula, in 1786. Nine years later they threw the Dutch out of Malacca to gain a second trading port.

At the age of twenty-four Thomas Stamford Raffles was posted by the East India Company to Prince of Wales Island as Assistant Secretary to the Governor. In 1811 he devised the military campaign that took Java from the Dutch. Appointed Lieutenant-Governor of Java, Raffles introduced wide-ranging reforms.

After a trip to England in 1816, Raffles became Lieutenant-Governor of Bencoolen (Bengkulu) in Sumatra. Here he developed a plan for a major trading port at Singapore, having realised its strategic importance.

Raffles landed at Singapore on 29 January 1819. He went to the local ruler, Temenggong Abdu'r Rahman, proposing a treaty. The Temenggong's superior, Sultan Hussein of Johor, agreed to Raffles' proposals on 6 February.

Some enthusiastic promotion among the merchants trading in India and China established Singapore as a trading port within twelve months. By 1824 its volume of trade had outstripped that of Prince of Wales Island.

The Straits Settlements

In 1826 Singapore, Malacca and Penang became the Straits Settlements, with their own governor. The era of the British East India Company ended in 1858, when Britain took direct control.

Malaya first grew rubber during the 1870s, and before long Malaya was the world's primary source. Singapore became the main port for its export. The opening of the Suez Canal in 1869 created an upsurge in the number of ships calling at Singapore.

The resultant prosperity made Singapore a magnet attracting people from other parts of Asia, particularly China. Europeans ran some large trading companies, but day-to-day commerce was handled by Chinese

Japan invades

Singapore was considered a bastion of British defence. Having pushed the British, Australian and Indian forces out of Malaya in 1941, the Japanese Imperial Army marched into Singapore on 15 February 1942.

Tens of thousands of allied troops were thrown into the Changi and Outram Road prisons

A group of Malay princes in Singapore in the nineteenth century

merchants. Upper-level government administrators were expatriates sent out from London.

For decades expatriates enjoyed a very pleasant lifestyle with servants and large houses. Wealthy Chinese merchant families did much the same. Life for the people who did the labouring and menial jobs was not so good — slum conditions with few facilities were their lot.

or shipped off to work in prisoner-of-war camps across Asia. The Japanese renamed the island Syonan (Light of the South).

While the experiences of military prisoners-of-war in Changi have been well documented, less

SYONAN
The name given to Singapore by the invading Japanese, meaning 'Light of the South'

Boat Quay was for decades the main arrival point of passengers and cargoes

is known of the plight of those Singaporeans who opposed the Japanese invasion. There were many brutal campaigns to weed out supposed anti-Japanese activists.

Having opposed Japan's invasion of China in 1937, Singapore's Chinese community suffered especially vicious treatment. Males aged eighteen to fifty years were routinely trucked to Changi beach to be shot by Japanese soldiers.

Members of the Malay and Indian communities were shipped to Thailand to work on the infamous Thai–Burma Railway. Indians who refused to join the Japanese-backed Indian National Army (INA) were executed.

Postwar changes

British forces had reoccupied Singapore in September 1945, placing it under military law for six months. On 1 April 1946 the Straits Settlements was formally disbanded and Singapore made a Crown Colony in its own right.

In July 1947 London authorised the setting up of Singaporean Executive and Legislative Councils, which would advise the Governor on the day-to-day running of the colony. Six members of the Legislative Council were elected by the people at Singapore's first election on 20 March 1948.

Later that year the growing struggle between Britain and the communist movement for control of Singapore and Malaya led to the declaration of a State of Emergency. Large numbers of troops were stationed in Singapore. British and Australian air forces flew bombing raids on communist positions in Malaya.

SCOTT BRODIE

Kranji War Cemetery, where Allied military personnel who died at Singapore are interred

Increasing nationalism

Following a review by Sir George Rendel, a new constitutional structure with expanded self-government came into effect. At the general election of 1955 David Marshall — leader of the Labor Front — became Chief Minister in a coalition government.

Attempts by the communists to render Marshall's government impotent came to a head on Thursday 12 May 1955. Bloody riots erupted when police attempted to break up picket lines of striking unionists. Four people died in the melée.

The government threatened to close three high schools if discipline was not re-established,

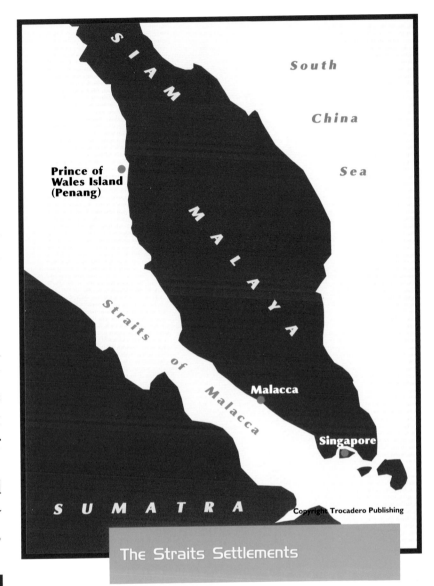

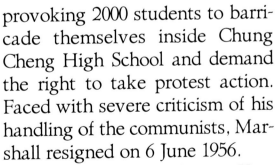

The Straits Settlements

provoking 2000 students to barricade themselves inside Chung Cheng High School and demand the right to take protest action. Faced with severe criticism of his handling of the communists, Marshall resigned on 6 June 1956.

He was replaced by Lim Yew Hok, who began deregistering communist-backed unions and the

David Marshall, leader of the Labor Front, was elected Singapore's first Chief Minister in 1955

Lim Yew Hok

The formation of Malaysia

Singapore believed its destiny lay in integrating with Malaya. Despite communist opposition, a referendum on 1 September 1962 voted overwhelmingly to merge with Malaya, Sarawak and British North Borneo (Sabah) to form Malaysia.

After the merger on 16 September 1963, President Sukarno of Indonesia launched his Konfrontasi (Confrontation) campaign in an attempt to destabilise Malaysia. The hostilities began eight days after Malaysia came into being, with a bomb blast at a Singapore hotel.

When Indonesian military forces staged sorties into Sarawak

students' union. A sit-in by students at Chung Cheng High School and the Chinese High School exploded into bloody riots on 25 October. For five days Singapore was under curfew. Thirteen people were killed, hundreds injured, and almost 1000 arrested.

Self-government

All-party delegations to London in 1957 and 1958 negotiated further self-government and a new constitution.

On 30 May 1959 more than 500 000 Singaporeans voted compulsorily. They elected the People's Action Party (PAP), led by Lee Kuan Yew, to forty-three of the fifty-one seats in the Parliament.

Police clash with student demonstrators in 1955

and Sabah, the task of defending the new nation fell primarily to the 50 000 British troops stationed there, assisted by Australian and New Zealand units.

Ethnic friction between the predominantly Chinese community of Singapore and the predominantly Malay community of Malaya caused friction in the new nation. Extremists, claiming Singapore treated its Malay minority as second-class citizens, began whipping up tension. In Singapore on 21 July 1964, fighting between cultural groups erupted into full-scale race riots that lasted almost a week. Twenty-three Singaporeans died and almost five hundred were injured.

Following further riots, on 6 August 1965 Tunku Abdul Rahman of Malaya advised Lee Kuan Yew it was essential Singapore leave Malaysia. Despite Lee's opposition, three days later the Malaysian Parliament voted to separate.

After Malaysia

Becoming a republic, a nation in its own right, proved a major turning point in Singapore's evolution. It embarked on an ambitious plan of economic and social development.

Confrontation with Indonesia ended on 12 August 1966, when Sukarno was deposed by the military led by General Suharto. One year later, Singapore, Malaysia, Indonesia, the Philippines and Thailand formed the Association of South-East Asian Nations (ASEAN).

Britain's 1968 announcement that it would withdraw all military forces from Singapore came as a major shock. Apart from the

One of the new schools constructed during the 1950s and 1960s

Escaping the humidity in the swimming pools in one of Singapore's many new town developments

WWW.SOURCES

www.knowledgenet.com.sg
Comprehensive historical items and data

www.sg/flavour/history.html
Singapore history

www.museum.org.sg
National Heritage Board

library.thinkquest.org/10414
Chronological history

www.scholars.nus.edu.sg/landow/post/
singapore/history/historyov.html
Links to history sites, archives

defence considerations, the British military employed 40 000 Singaporeans directly. The loss of these jobs would have a profound effect on the economy.

Modernising and growing

Singapore embarked on a program of growth and development that would eventually make it one of the strongest economies in Asia.

The energy of the multiracial, multilingual population was harnessed very effectively in a single-minded drive to create a better life for all citizens. International companies established manufacturing plants in Singapore, creating jobs and new opportunities. As well, many Singaporean industries began marketing their goods and services around the world.

A massive housing development program saw the old near-slum conditions, in which many poorer Singaporeans lived, swept away. People were relocated into high-rise flats in new estates across the island. While in other parts of the world such housing has often degenerated into slums, in Singapore it appears to have worked well.

Statistics

Total population
4 300 419
Birth rate
12.8 per 1000 population
Death rate
4.2 per 1000 population
Infant mortality rate
3.6 per 1000 live births
Life expectancy
male 77, female 83

GDP growth rate **10.1%**
GDP per capita **US$26 500**
GDP by sector
industry **30%**
services **70%**
Government revenues
US$18 billion
Government expenditures
US$17 billion

Labour force **2.1 million**
Labour force by sector
financial, business and
other services **35%**
manufacturing **21%**
construction **13%**
transport and
communication **9%**
Unemployment rate **3%**

Land area
647.5 sq. km
Lowest point
Singapore Strait — sea level
Highest point
Bukit Timah — 166 m

Major exports
**machinery and equipment,
electronic equipment,
electronic components,
chemicals, mineral fuels**

COPYRIGHT TROCADERO PUBLISHING

Singapore's national flag comprises two horizontal bands, red and white, and features a crescent moon and five stars. The red symbolises universal brotherhood and the equality of humankind; the white stands for purity and virtue. The crescent moon denotes a rising young nation; and the five stars represent progress, peace, democracy, equality and justice.

Secondary industries
**electronics, chemicals,
financial services,
oil drilling equipment,
petroleum refining,
rubber processing,
rubber products,
processed food, beverages,
ship repair,
entrepôt trade, biotechnology**

Official national
language **Malay**
Other official languages
Mandarin, English, Tamil
Currency **Singapore dollar**
Religions **Buddhism, Islam,
Christianity, Hinduism, Taoism**

Index

Focus on Asia: Singapore   ISBN 0 86415 425 9
Published by   Franklin Watts 96 Leonard Street   London EC2A4XD
Created and produced by Trocadero Publishing   Copyright © 2002 S and L Brodie   Printed in Hong Kong